W9-AQO-871

First Drawings
AIRPLANES

ABDO
Publishing Company

A Buddy Book by Maria Hosley

VISIT US AT
www.abdopublishing.com

Published by ABDO Publishing Company, 4940 Viking Drive, Edina, Minnesota 55435.

Copyright © 2007 by Abdo Consulting Group, Inc. International copyrights reserved in all countries. No part of this book may be reproduced in any form without written permission from the publisher. Buddy Books™ is a trademark and logo of ABDO Publishing Company.

Printed in the United States.

Editor: Sarah Tieck
Contributing Editor: Michael P. Goecke
Graphic Design: Maria Hosley
Illustrations: Maria Hosley
Interior Photographs: Photos.com

Library of Congress Cataloging-in-Publication Data

Hosley, Maria.
   Airplanes / Maria Hosley.
      p. cm. — (First Drawings)
   Includes index.
   ISBN-13: 978-1-59679-799-4
   ISBN-10: 1-59679-799-1
   1. Airplanes in art—Juvenile literature. 2. Pencil drawing—Technique—Juvenile literature. I. Title.

NC825.A4H67 2007
743'.8962913334—dc22

2006034580

Table Of Contents

Getting Started

Today you're going to learn to draw an airplane. Not sure you know how to draw? If you know how to make circles, squares, and triangles, you can draw most anything!

You will learn to draw in four steps. First, you will measure to get the correct sizes. Next, you will lightly draw the basic shapes. This helps you construct an airplane. From those basic shapes, you will make the final outline. And last, you will erase the basic shape lines and add **detail**.

Can you see the basic shapes in the picture of the real airplane?

To draw an airplane, you'll need paper, a sharpened pencil, a big eraser, and a hard, flat surface. Many artists like to draw at a table or a desk. They sit up straight with their tools in front of them. Gather your supplies. Then, let's get started!

ARTIST'S TOOLBOX

Airplanes come in many different shapes and sizes. So, you may want to find a **reference** picture. Many artists draw from these images. Some have folders filled with them!

Start your own reference folder by collecting photographs or pictures from magazines. Then, use them as you draw. This book has a reference picture of an airplane to get you started.

REFERENCE PICTURES

Measurements and Proportions

Have you ever looked at a drawing and thought about whether it looks real? Many people draw airplanes that look real.

To make a **realistic** drawing of an airplane, find out its proportions. Proportion is the size of one thing compared to another. For example, an airplane's wings should be a size that fits with the body. Using correct proportions helps make your airplane drawing look realistic.

There's an easy way to match the proportions of an airplane for your drawing. You can use strips of paper to measure the parts on your **reference** picture. Here's how to do it:

Cut a strip of paper the same width as the airplane's engine. Then cut several more strips of the same size.

Lay the strips on the airplane. Do this to compare the engine size with the length of the top wings and the airplane's height.

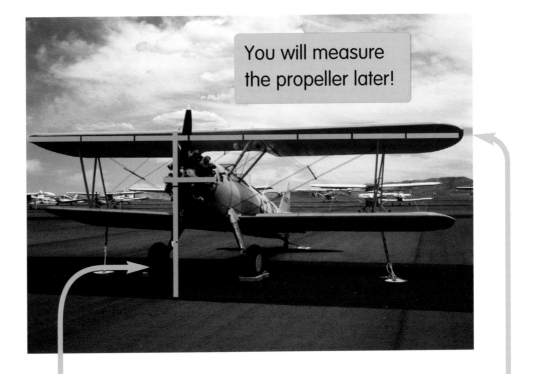

You will measure the propeller later!

The plane's height is a little less than 3 strips high.

The wings are about 8 strips wide.

Choosing A Size For Your Drawing

To draw this airplane at this size, cut several strips of paper that match the length of the orange strips shown above.

If you want a larger drawing, cut longer strips. And if you want a smaller drawing, cut shorter strips. Just make sure the strips fit on your drawing paper.

Place your cut strips on your drawing paper. Arrange them so they match the reference picture. With your pencil, lightly mark the ends of each strip.

Add another mark here because the airplane is shorter than 3 strips.

Basic Shapes

All things are easier to draw if you break them down into basic shapes. Draw these shapes *very lightly*. They are only a guide that you will erase later. And when the lines are light, it is easy to erase and try again. Remember to use your proportion lines as a guide!

Between the engine guidelines, draw a circle. Put in ovals for the ends of each wing. Then, connect them from end to end. **Sketch** circles for the wheels. Draw a long, slanted oval to form the body. Finally, sketch lines for the wing **braces** and the wheel bars.

Leaving the strips on the reference picture will help you position your shapes.

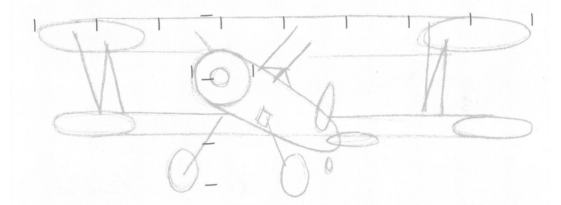

You will draw the propeller last. This way, you can choose to make the propeller moving or still.

Final Outline

Now you have the basic shapes for your airplane! You can use them to make the final outline shape. Do this *lightly* with a pencil.

Follow around the outside of the basic shapes. Add lines to shape the wing **braces**, the wheel bars, and the engine.

It's time to add the propeller. Is your airplane flying in the air or parked on the ground? When an airplane is in the air, its propeller spins quickly. So, it is hard to see. But when an airplane is parked, you can clearly see the propeller.

Adding Detail

Once you are happy with your outline, erase the basic shape lines. Be careful not to erase any lines you still need.

Now you can add **details**. **Sketch** in lines for the propellers and the engine. Add lines for the edges of the wings. Draw small boxes where the wheel bars attach to the body. Finally, put in the windshield.

When you are happy with your outline and **details**, you can make them darker. Do this with your pencil or a marker. Erase any extra lines, and you're done!

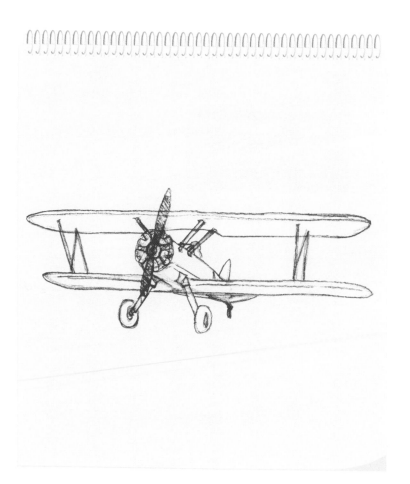

Keep Drawing

You have now finished a drawing of an airplane. Good job! Use these steps next time you want to draw something.

Don't worry if drawing feels like a challenge at first. Like anything else, drawing takes practice.

Have fun with your new skills. And remember to practice, practice, practice! The more you draw the better you will become.

Want to add to your drawing? Try using watercolor paints to add color to your airplane. Add a background to your drawing, too.

Start painting with light colors.
Add more color in the shadow
areas. These details help shape
the airplane and make it look
realistic.

Caricature Airplanes

It is fun to **exaggerate** parts of the airplane. This is how you make a caricature. A caricature is a picture that looks like a cartoon.

Pick one feature of the airplane. Then, exaggerate it to make it look funny. Just use your imagination!

You can make an airplane have human **expressions**. Practice making airplane faces that show emotion. Then, try making your airplane's body position match its mood.

SLEEPY

happy

By using the same basic shapes, we created a caricature of the airplane. We tilted the wings, and added wide eyes and an open mouth. These details make the airplane look unsteady.

Important Words

brace parts of the airplane that help strengthen the wing.

detail a minor decoration, such as an airplane's spinning propeller.

exaggerate to make something seem larger than it really is.

expression a look that shows feeling.

realistic showing things as they are in real life.

reference a picture or an item used for information or help.

sketch to make a rough drawing.

Web Sites

To learn more about drawing airplanes, visit ABDO Publishing Company on the World Wide Web. Web site links about drawing airplanes are featured on our Book Links page. These links are routinely monitored and updated to provide the most current information available.

www.abdopublishing.com

Index